JAZZ PIANO SOLOS VOLUME 59

west coast jazz

Arranged by Brent Edstrom

contents

ISBN 978-1-5400-4794-6

Visit Hal Leonard Online at
www.halleonard.com

Contact us:
Hal Leonard
7777 West Bluemound Road
Milwaukee, WI 53213
Email: info@halleonard.com

In Europe, contact:
Hal Leonard Europe Limited
42 Wigmore Street
Marylebone, London, W1U 2RN
Email: info@halleonardeurope.com

In Australia, contact:
Hal Leonard Australia Pty. Ltd.
4 Lentara Court
Cheltenham, Victoria, 3192 Australia
Email: info@halleonard.com.au

AH MOORE

By AL COHN

BERNIE'S TUNE

By BERNIE MILLER

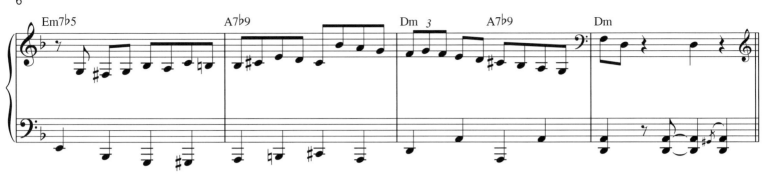

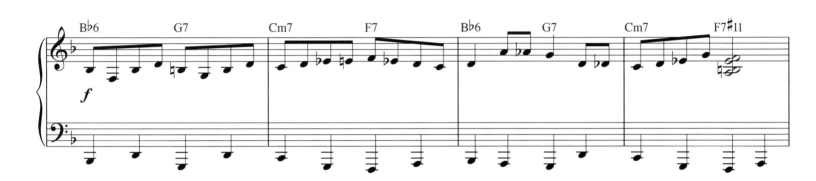

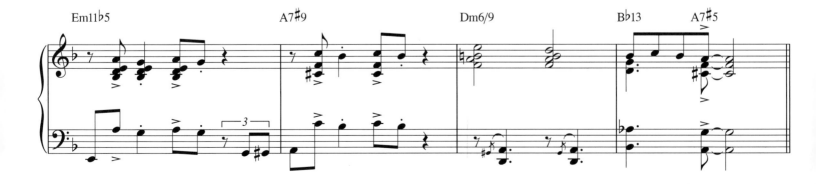

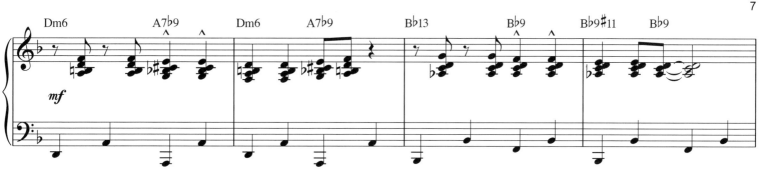

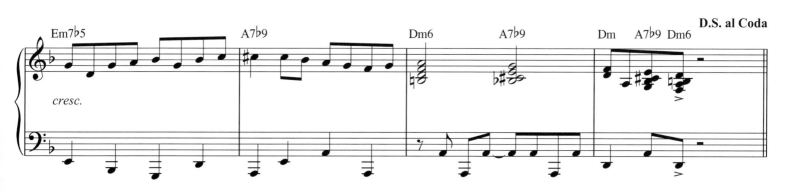

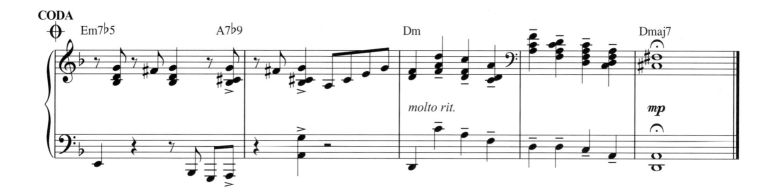

BLUES MOOD

By KENNY CLARKE

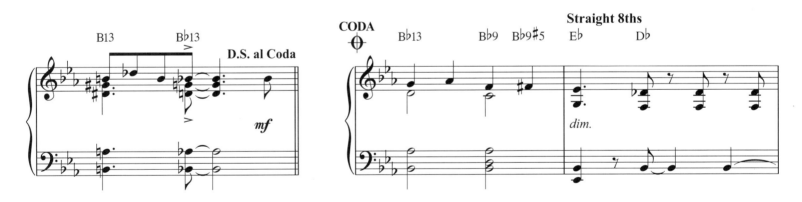

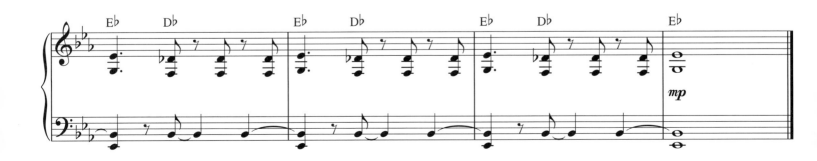

GINZA SAMBA

By VINCE GUARALDI

COMES LOVE

Words and Music by LEW BROWN,
CHARLES TOBIAS and SAM STEPT

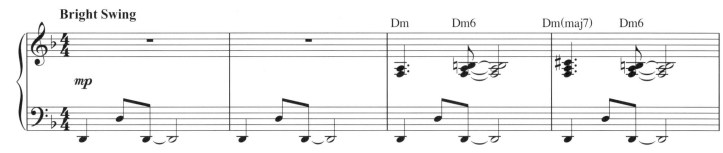

Arrangement based on one by Conte Candoli

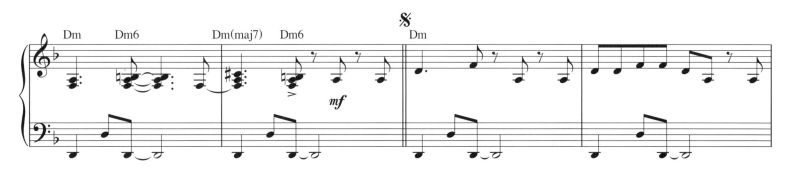

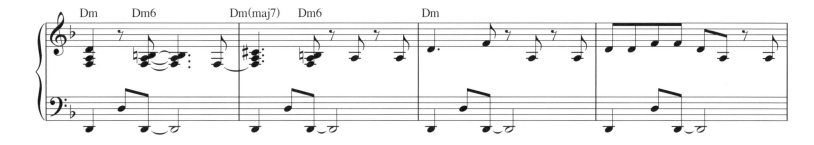

EAST OF THE SUN
(And West of the Moon)

Words and Music by
BROOKS BOWMAN

23

FENWYCK'S FARFEL

By VINCE GUARALDI

Moderate Swing

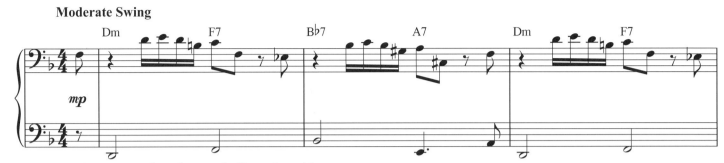

Arrangement based on one by Vince Guaraldi

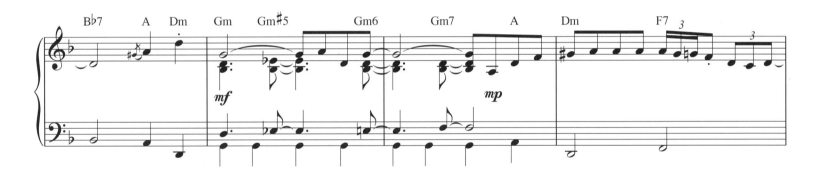

LH like a strummed guitar

LINE FOR LYONS

By GERRY MULLIGAN

Based on a version by Gerry Mulligan and Chet Baker

To Coda

THE MORNING AFTER

By CHICO HAMILTON

35

MY OLD FLAME

Words and Music by ARTHUR JOHNSTON
and SAM COSLOW

SOFT SHOE

By GERRY MULLIGAN

Arrangement based on one by Chet Baker and Stan Getz

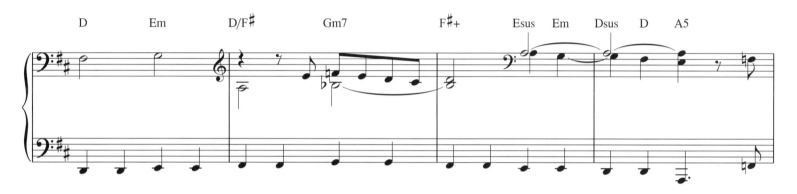

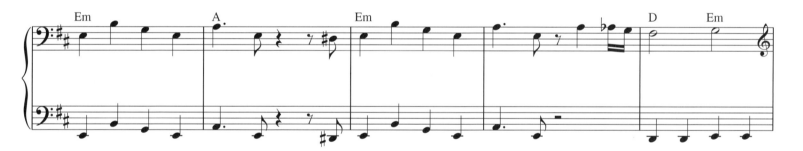

NOT REALLY THE BLUES

By JOHNNY MANDEL

OF THEE I SING

Music and Lyrics by GEORGE GERSHWIN
and IRA GERSHWIN

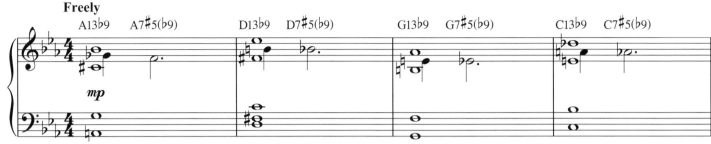

Based on an arrangement by Stan Getz

To Coda ⊕

OH PLAY THAT THING

By SHORTY ROGERS

52

SOFTLY AS IN A MORNING SUNRISE

Lyrics by OSCAR HAMMERSTEIN II
Music by SIGMUND ROMBERG

Medium Swing

Arrangement based on one by Bud Shank

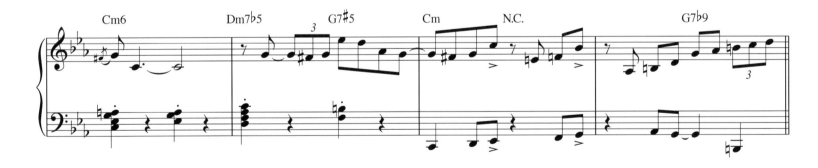

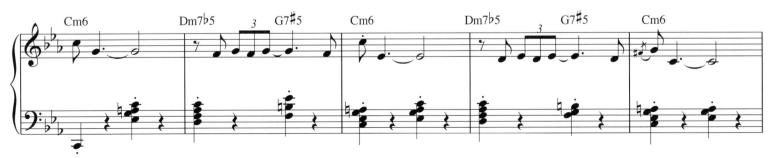

SONOR
(a/k/a Sonar)

By KENNY CLARKE
and GERALD WIGGINS

Bright Swing

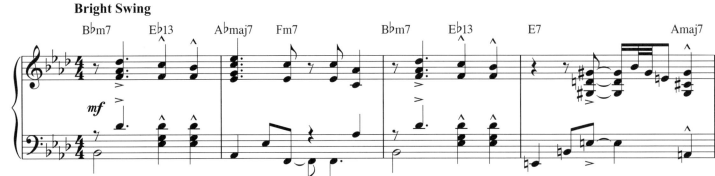

Arrangement based on one by Victor Feldman

SUDDENLY IT'S SPRING

Words by JOHNNY BURKE
Music by JAMES VAN HEUSEN

Arragement based on one by Stan Getz

To Coda ⊕

D.S. al Coda

TOPSY

Words and Music by EDGAR BATTLE
and EDDIE DURHAM

Medium uptempo Swing

WAILING VESSEL

By BOB COOPER

Arrangement based on one by Bud Shank

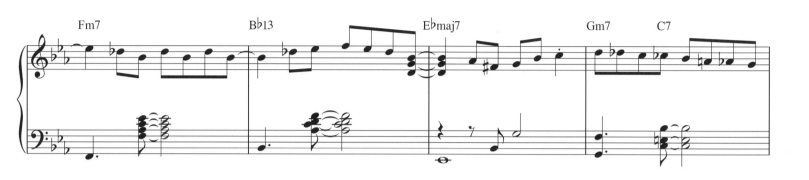

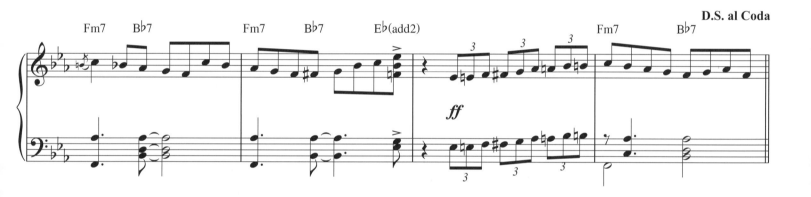

WALKIN' SHOES

By GERRY MULLIGAN

Arrangement based on one by Gerry Mulligan

To Coda ⊕

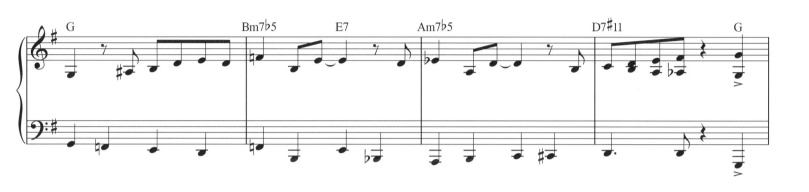

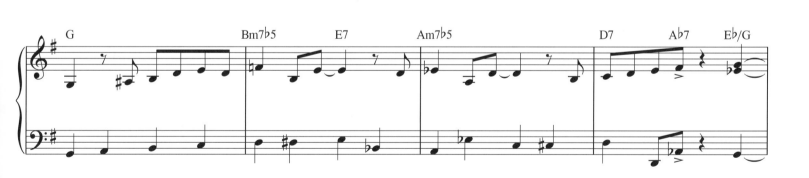

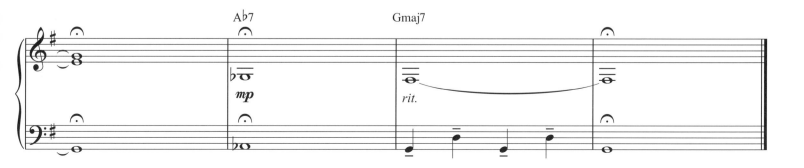

WEST COAST BLUES

By JOHN L. (WES) MONTGOMERY

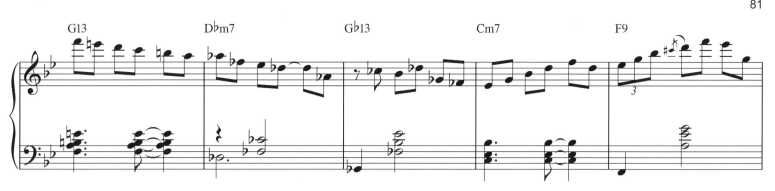

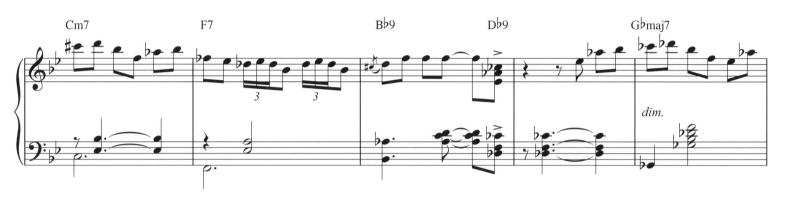

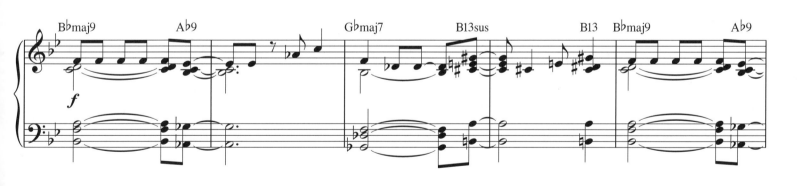

THE TRAIN AND THE RIVER

By JIMMY GIUFFRE

The Best-Selling Jazz Book of All Time Is Now Legal!

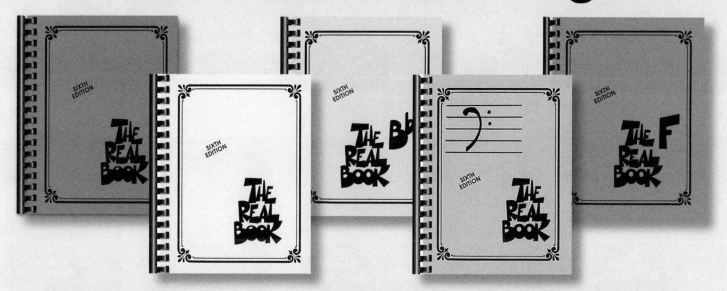

The Real Books are the most popular jazz books of all time. Since the 1970s, musicians have trusted these volumes to get them through every gig, night after night. The problem is that the books were illegally produced and distributed, without any regard to copyright law, or royalties paid to the composers who created these musical masterpieces.

Hal Leonard is very proud to present the first legitimate and legal editions of these books ever produced. You won't even notice the difference, other than all the notorious errors being fixed: the covers and typeface look the same, the song lists are nearly identical, and the price for our edition is even cheaper than the originals!

VOLUME 1

00240221	C Edition	$39.99
00240224	B♭ Edition	$39.99
00240225	E♭ Edition	$39.99
00240226	Bass Clef Edition	$39.99
00286389	F Edition	$39.99
00240292	C Edition 6 x 9	$35.00
00240339	B♭ Edition 6 x 9	$35.00
00147792	Bass Clef Edition 6 x 9	$35.00
00451087	C Edition on CD-ROM	$29.99
00200984	Online Backing Tracks: Selections	$45.00
00110604	Book/USB Flash Drive Backing Tracks Pack	$79.99
00110599	USB Flash Drive Only	$50.00

VOLUME 2

00240222	C Edition	$39.99
00240227	B♭ Edition	$39.99
00240228	E♭ Edition	$39.99
00240229	Bass Clef Edition	$39.99
00240293	C Edition 6 x 9	$35.00
00125900	B♭ Edition 6 x 9	$35.00
00451088	C Edition on CD-ROM	$30.99
00125900	The Real Book – Mini Edition	$35.00
00204126	Backing Tracks on USB Flash Drive	$50.00
00204131	C Edition – USB Flash Drive Pack	$79.99

VOLUME 3

00240233	C Edition	$39.99
00240284	B♭ Edition	$39.99
00240285	E♭ Edition	$39.99
00240286	Bass Clef Edition	$39.99
00240338	C Edition 6 x 9	$35.00
00451089	C Edition on CD-ROM	$29.99

VOLUME 4

00240296	C Edition	$39.99
00103348	B♭ Edition	$39.99
00103349	E♭ Edition	$39.99
00103350	Bass Clef Edition	$39.99

VOLUME 5

00240349	C Edition	$39.99
00175278	B♭ Edition	$39.99
00175279	E♭ Edition	$39.99

VOLUME 6

00240534	C Edition	$39.99
00223637	E♭ Edition	$39.99

Also available:

00151290	The Real Book – Enhanced Chords	$29.99
00282973	The Reharmonized Real Book	$39.99

Complete song lists online at www.halleonard.com

Prices, content, and availability subject to change without notice.

THE REAL BOOK MULTI-TRACKS

TODAY'S BEST WAY TO PRACTICE JAZZ! Accurate, easy-to-read lead sheets and professional, customizable audio tracks accessed online for 10 songs

1. MAIDEN VOYAGE PLAY-ALONG

Autumn Leaves • Blue Bossa • Doxy • Footprints • Maiden Voyage • Now's the Time • On Green Dolphin Street • Satin Doll • Summertime • Tune Up.
00196616 Book with Online Media...........$17.99

2. MILES DAVIS PLAY-ALONG

Blue in Green • Boplicity (Be Bop Lives) • Four • Freddie Freeloader • Milestones • Nardis • Seven Steps to Heaven • So What • Solar • Walkin'.
00196798 Book with Online Media $17.99

3. ALL BLUES PLAY-ALONG

All Blues • Back at the Chicken Shack • Billie's Bounce (Bill's Bounce) • Birk's Works • Blues by Five • C-Jam Blues • Mr. P.C. • One for Daddy-O • Reunion Blues • Turnaround.
00196692 Book with Online Media $17.99

4. CHARLIE PARKER PLAY-ALONG

Anthropology • Blues for Alice • Confirmation • Donna Lee • K.C. Blues • Moose the Mooche • My Little Suede Shoes • Ornithology • Scrapple from the Apple • Yardbird Suite.
00196799 Book with Online Media $17.99

5. JAZZ FUNK PLAY-ALONG

Alligator Bogaloo • The Chicken • Cissy Strut • Cold Duck Time • Comin' Home Baby • Mercy, Mercy, Mercy • Put It Where You Want It • Sidewinder • Tom Cat • Watermelon Man.
00196728 Book with Online Media $17.99

6. SONNY ROLLINS PLAY-ALONG

Airegin • Blue Seven • Doxy • Duke of Iron • Oleo • Pent up House • St. Thomas • Sonnymoon for Two • Strode Rode • Tenor Madness.
00218264 Book with Online Media $17.99

7. THELONIOUS MONK PLAY-ALONG

Bemsha Swing • Blue Monk • Bright Mississippi • Green Chimneys • Monk's Dream • Reflections • Rhythm-a-ning • 'Round Midnight • Straight No Chaser • Ugly Beauty.
00232768 Book with Online Media $17.99

8. BEBOP ERA PLAY-ALONG

Au Privave • Boneology • Bouncing with Bud • Dexterity • Groovin' High • Half Nelson • In Walked Bud • Lady Bird • Move • Witches Pit.
00196728 Book with Online Media $17.99

9. CHRISTMAS CLASSICS PLAY-ALONG

Blue Christmas • Christmas Time Is Here • Frosty the Snow Man • Have Yourself a Merry Little Christmas • I'll Be Home for Christmas • My Favorite Things • Santa Claus Is Comin' to Town • Silver Bells • White Christmas • Winter Wonderland.
00236808 Book with Online Media..........$17.99

10. CHRISTMAS SONGS PLAY-ALONG

Away in a Manger • The First Noel • Go, Tell It on the Mountain • Hark! the Herald Angels Sing • Jingle Bells • Joy to the World • O Come, All Ye Faithful • O Holy Night • Up on the Housetop • We Wish You a Merry Christmas.
00236809 Book with Online Media..........$17.99

11. JOHN COLTRANE PLAY-ALONG

Blue Train (Blue Trane) • Central Park West • Cousin Mary • Giant Steps • Impressions • Lazy Bird • Moment's Notice • My Favorite Things • Naima (Niema) • Syeeda's Song Flute.
00275624 Book with Online Media $17.99

12. 1950S JAZZ PLAY-ALONG

Con Alma • Django • Doodlin' • In Your Own Sweet Way • Jeru • Jordu • Killer Joe • Lullaby of Birdland • Night Train • Waltz for Debby.
00275647 Book with Online Media $17.99

13. 1960S JAZZ PLAY-ALONG

Ceora • Dat Dere • Dolphin Dance • Equinox • Jeannine • Recorda Me • Stolen Moments • Tom Thumb • Up Jumped Spring • Windows.
00275651 Book with Online Media $17.99

14. 1970S JAZZ PLAY-ALONG

Birdland • Bolivia • Chameleon • 500 Miles High • Lucky Southern • Phase Dance • Red Baron • Red Clay • Spain • Sugar.
00275652 Book with Online Media $17.99

15. CHRISTMAS TUNES PLAY-ALONG

The Christmas Song (Chestnuts Roasting on an Open Fire) • Do You Hear What I Hear • Feliz Navidad • Here Comes Santa Claus (Right down Santa Claus Lane) • A Holly Jolly Christmas • Let It Snow! Let It Snow! Let It Snow! • The Little Drummer Boy • The Most Wonderful Time of the Year • Rudolph the Red-Nosed Reindeer • Sleigh Ride.
00278073 Book with Online Media $17.99

HAL•LEONARD®
www.halleonard.com

Prices, content and availability subject to change without notice.